SURVIVING THE TSUNAMI OF GRIEF

FOR THE BEREAVED AND THOSE WANTING TO SUPPORT THEM

KATRINA TAEE AND WENDELIEN MCNICOLL
WITH ILLUSTRATIONS BY RUTH THORP

To all the clients who trusted us to accompany them along their journey through grief and to both our families, who support us in what we do.

FOREWORD

BY BARONESS JULIA NEUBERGER

Surviving The Tsunami of Grief is a book we all need. We need it when we are suddenly hit by loss, death and grief. We need it when we are trying to help someone we love, or know, come to terms with loss. We need it to prepare ourselves for when the time for grieving comes for us, if one ever can. We need it because our society finds grief so very hard to talk about. We have no formula to greet someone newly bereaved, like the Irish "I'm sorry for your troubles." We no longer wear a black armband or black in general so people know we are grieving. We have few rituals and no words. Locked into wordlessness and lack of ritual is deep despair, anger, rage and a kind of suffering that makes people think they are going mad. A veritable tsunami. This book will not, cannot solve it for you but it can help you and yours find their way and it can guide you to where help is to be found. It is sensitive, comprehensive and kind, it speaks in the words of the bereaved who can really help heal the broken-hearted and it needs to be read and digested by us all.

Surviving The Tsunami of Grief

Written by Katrina Taee and Wendelien McNicoll

Illustrated by Ruth Thorp

Published by NewAct Publishing

Illustrator: Ruth Thorp www.ruththorpstudio.co.uk

Book Design: Rhizome Consulting www.rhizomeconsulting.com

Book Production: York Publishing Services www.yps-publishing.co.uk

Book Distribution: York Publishing Services www.ypdbooks.com
                        +44 (0) 1904 431213

ISBN: 978-1-9162884-0-9

CONTENTS

INTRODUCTION

We have created this book for those of you who are facing the daunting journey through grief and for the people who are supporting you. We want to help you make sense of one of the most barren, confusing and difficult times you may ever face in your life. It can be a solitary time and even in company you can feel infinitely alone. Grief can be all-consuming at times and it can be hard to see a way forward or indeed to understand exactly what is happening or how to make sense of it. This book is not a checklist for grief or for how you should or should not feel. What we have tried to do is to illustrate just how many different ways there are of expressing grief but these are by no means all. Our book supports you in not letting your feelings be stifled by others. After all, why shouldn't or wouldn't you feel the way that you do, or express yourself in whatever way you wish?

In the first half of the book (chapters 1-8) we use the visual metaphor of a tsunami to explain what can happen when people grieve. We have painted a picture which may resonate with many of your experiences, to enlighten your own journey through grief and to provide insight to those kind and concerned people who offer you love and support. We have kept the book deliberately concise because we know that in the early stages of grief you may find it hard to concentrate; reading can require a lot of effort at a time when you may be feeling fatigued and overwhelmed. The raw physicality of grief is often overlooked or misunderstood. We hope this is a book you and others can dip in and out of when needed.

In the second half of the book (chapters 9-11) we offer ways in which those wishing to help you can do so in a useful and comprehensive way, according to their own talents, capabilities, comfort zones and strengths. Those three chapters can also be used by you, the bereaved, as a way of recognising and sourcing the different types of help and support you may want or need. We believe it will offer you encouragement to ask for anything that will make life a bit easier at that particular moment when you need help the most.

We have had the privilege of working with many wonderful clients. They have shared their painful and dark days with us, as well as their small steps forward and their triumphs when they have overcome adversity. We have seen them as they journey towards a new and different life, without the person who died. This book is about what our clients have taught us through their encounters with grief. We would like to share it with you to help you navigate your way through bereavement with the reassurance of our own personal and professional experience.

2019 Katrina Taee and Wendelien McNicoll

CHAPTER 1
LIFE AS YOU KNOW IT

You know this beach so well, the ebb and flow of the tide, the view and the feel of sand under your feet. This may remind you of how your life was before the death of your loved one.

The words people use to describe their life before their bereavement are, amongst others: normal, usual, calm, ordinary, everyday, boring, with ups and downs, secure, fun, shared, safe, loving and predictable.

How would you describe your life at that time?

CHAPTER 2

THE CAUSE OF THE TSUNAMI

Sadly, we know that death comes in different guises. It may be through the natural progression of old age or illness. It may have been an awful accident or an unexpected death. Perhaps there was a miscarriage, a stillbirth or the death of a child. It could have been murder at the hand of another or death due to an act of terrorism. Perhaps someone died by suicide. For those in the Armed Forces or Emergency Services, death could have occurred in the line of duty.

Yet each person's reaction to the death of someone they have loved or have been friends with is a unique experience to him or her.

We know that foundations are shaken and rocked to the core.

CHAPTER 3

THE RECEDING SEA

In the days following the death, it can feel as if the beach you knew so well is disappearing before your eyes. As the sea recedes, just as it does at the start of a tsunami, your beach may become unrecognisable to you and you are not sure what is happening to you.

We know this can be a very shocking, troubling and deeply upsetting time which can feel very unstable and bewildering.

I can't believe I'm not going to see him again

DISBELIEF

It's not possible

It can't be true

How did this happen to us?

Time holds no meaning now

Why, why me, why us?

What am I going to do?

No-one can help me

It's like a bad dream

I think I am going mad

I feel the need to go over and over what happened

I can't believe I feel so relieved he died

I 'saw' him today – a moment's joy then devastation that it wasn't him

SHOCK

I can't sleep

I feel sick

I hate waking up and remembering

I'm not getting up in the mornings

Sometimes I don't get dressed

I can't stop crying

I can't cry

I can't breathe

I feel wobbly

I feel frozen

I don't feel like I can swallow

I can't eat

I make myself eat even when I don't want to

I'm OK then I'm not OK

I am not functioning very well

I am not sure what I am thinking or feeling

I am overwhelmed

I am so angry he left us

There has to be an autopsy but I don't understand why

I hate waking up
and remembering

It can't be true

DENIAL

This did not happen

Any minute now he will come through the door

I am coping all right

I don't need help

I can't do this

I can't take it in

I don't want to talk to anyone – if I did, it might be true

I saw her body but she's not dead – she can't be

Someone must be to blame

NUMBNESS AND/OR HEIGHTENED SENSITIVITY

I don't feel anything – I feel everything acutely

I feel paralysed – I feel restless

I haven't cried – I cry all the time

I cannot take in anything people say – I explode at the slightest thing people say

I'm in a dark place – everything glares at me too brightly

I feel flat – I feel hyper

I am numb – I feel very scared

FEELING AS THOUGH IN A 'FOG'

I feel like I have landed on an alien planet

I feel as if I am wading through mud

My legs/body feel heavy

I cannot concentrate

I feel so muddled

I feel as if I am on the periphery of something

I don't think I am driving very well

I feel bone-weary

GOING THROUGH THE MOTIONS

I am on automatic pilot

I am doing what needs to be done

It feels so hard to make any sort of decision

My body remembers what to do

My brain is trying hard to keep up

I am a zombie, a robot

I can't concentrate

CHAPTER 4

THE POWERFUL SURGE OF THE INCOMING WAVE

While you are still reeling from the shock of the death, the waves of the tsunami come surging in through your beach and you find yourself struggling to stay afloat above the maelstrom. Every fibre of your body is experiencing the loss and it is affecting everything.

This is a time when you can feel truly overwhelmed by the loss, as it manifests itself in every area of your life. This is the time our clients mention the words the 'tsunami of grief' to us the most. During this daunting period, difficulties which your loved one may have helped you cope with, or issues you may never have spoken about before, can surface.

This is entirely normal and expected.

THE PHYSICAL MANIFESTATIONS

I feel exhausted

I feel paralysed

I feel inert

I feel heavy

I feel sick all the time

I can't eat (am losing weight)

I am eating too much (have gained weight)

I'm drinking too much

I just want to be touched

I know I am working too much but it helps me forget

I feel as if I've lost a limb

My heart aches all the time (it physically hurts)

I have a hole in my heart

I feel I have got a stone in my stomach

I feel physically anxious

My heart is beating too fast

I think I am having panic attacks

I am screaming, howling, crying, whimpering, sobbing...

I am in pain

I take drugs to block it out

I feel as if I have
lost a limb

I just want to curl up
under the duvet

I am smoking too much

Sometimes I am reckless, like driving too fast

I am sure I have the same illness as...

I look old

I have gone grey

I have got lead in my legs

I keep going to the GP – I think I need antidepressants

I have insomnia

I am withdrawing

I don't do emotional stuff at the moment

I get caught out when I least expect it and hate it when people see me cry

I watch TV till I fall asleep

I miss the intimacy of sex

I am having casual sex because I want to feel wanted again

My libido has gone

I am harming myself

I can't concentrate

I cannot remember anything

I scream alongside loud music in the car

I notice I am talking too much, too fast

I laugh nervously

THE EMOTIONAL IMPACT

Things are much harder now than they were at the beginning

I still see him in the bed, suffering – I can't get it out of my head

I am so lonely

I feel sad, angry, guilty, ashamed, scared, relieved, down, depressed, stuck, confused, overwhelmed, despairing, isolated, ashamed, vulnerable, flooded (and any other feeling you could name)

I feel unable to cope

I am in limbo

I am screaming inside – no-one knows what I am going through

I am yearning for him

I have got a Mum-shaped hole in my life now

I feel burdened because there is so much to do

I am tearful a lot of the time

If I start crying I will never stop

I wish I could have a really good cry

I feel as if I am drowning

It feels like I am in a tsunami of grief

I feel I am drifting

I am engulfed

I try to keep busy so I don't feel anything

I feel in constant anticipation of being overwhelmed by grief

I am struggling to cope with other people's grief/emotions

I can't seem to support my sister, as the grief over my niece, her child, gets in the way

I can't cope with my parents' grief – she was my child, not theirs

I don't care if something were to happen to me

I'm afraid of:

Going mad

Not being able to cope

The future

Losing control

People getting fed up with my anger

Dying myself

Losing someone else close to me

Supporting other family members

Ageing

Getting sick

Growing old alone

Being in the dark now

Being on my own

I feel anxious

I am a failure

A secret that I have kept under wraps for so long is spilling out

The 'what ifs' and 'if onlys' are eating me up

I still cannot believe it – I didn't even like him, so why do I feel like this?

Music is abhorrent to me – it upsets me

I see the negative in everything

No one can help me

Is this going to last for ever?

I pretend it did not happen

I am wearing a mask

How do I move on?

It would have been better if it had been me

I hate him for doing this to me

I can't say the word 'died'

Why did she leave me?

I am dying inside

I don't want to live without him

I want to join her

My own death is an option – it's my back-up plan

I laughed the other day and then I felt guilty

If I don't think about her I feel guilty

She knew my secret

I feel other people are forgetting her already but I am not

I think I killed him by not going to the doctor sooner

I think I killed him by giving him more painkillers

I long to talk
to her again

THE SOCIAL IMPLICATIONS

My circumstances are radically changing – I don't want them to

I hate empty enquiries as to how I am

Nobody can make it right for me

Don't assume because he was elderly, it makes his death OK

Only people who have lost someone can understand how I feel

My husband is a hero and I have to live up to that

My lover died but I cannot speak about it because he was married

I don't want to celebrate Christmas (or any other religious or celebratory festival)

I am dreading his birthday

I can't bear it that our wedding anniversary is coming up

I cannot go to another funeral

I cannot grieve for anyone else

My husband has started 'doing' a lot but I can't do that

My wife cries all the time and I cannot deal with it

I can't face going out with other couples

No-one invites me to dinner any more

People don't want to talk to me – I feel like a social pariah

An acquaintance crossed the road when she saw me coming

I don't want to stand at the school gates any more making small talk

I don't like telling people he died of AIDS

I can't mention the suicide – it makes people uncomfortable

No-one mentions the suicide – it's so awkward

I have started thinking about my abortion – I wish I hadn't had one

I feel like no-one wants to hear my grief

I am worried people are put off by my simmering anger

I am going to be so badly off now

I will never go on holiday again

Life looks like one long empty space now

I will never marry again

I will never have another child

Would you believe it, men are hitting on me?

I hated him, you know, so why can't I let go?

My sister was my best friend and confidante

My daughter-in-law does not allow me to see the grandchildren

As an ex-partner, I am excluded

Why am I grieving when I clearly did not love him?

I just needed a break from grief to pretend it did not happen

I wanted to be normal for a bit

THE PRACTICAL IMPLICATIONS

I want someone to tell me what to do

I dread coming back to the empty house

I keep double-checking the doors and windows are locked

I can't cook – she did all that

I can't do the finances – I never did that

I can't face opening the mail

I must get a job now

I got rid of everything that was hers straight away

I haven't touched his things – they are just as they were

I want her friends to have a 'piece of her' by giving them a personal item that belonged to her

The ashes are still at the crematorium/undertakers

I have secretly kept some of the ashes after the scattering

I have the ashes in my bedroom and cannot bear to part from them

I go to the grave every day – is that too frequent?

I haven't been to the grave since the funeral – I cannot face it/don't want to

I have covered the wall with his photos – they comfort me

I listen to his voice on the answering machine over and over again

I don't watch television, just endlessly channel hop

My Mum helped me make a memory box of my Dad's things

I wear his pyjamas at night

I smell her sweaters

I wear his aftershave

I can't sleep in the marital bed

I don't go in that room

I am
overwhelmed keeping
everything going

Things keep
'setting me off

The room is left exactly as it was when she died

I want my sister's room but my parents went mad

I want answers...

There is so much admin to do

How do I deal with his digital legacy – like his social media, photos and music?

I can't cope with my job

I hate crying in public

I must keep it together

My friends expect too much from me

My friendship group is drifting apart

I am never going to 'that' place ever again

I sit in her chair

The will is causing so many problems in the family

We cannot agree on anything

I have plenty of people to do something with but no-one to do nothing with

Weekends are the worst – everyone is busy with their families

Who can I go on holiday with now?

The joy has gone out of cooking and food

I cannot get used to cooking for one

I have to move out of my house

I have to clear her flat very quickly for re-rental

I cannot face clearing the house

I regret getting rid of her stuff so quickly

I cannot part with his things – they mean too much

My sisters both have children, so I have to look after Dad now – I feel responsible for him

I feel I can't start grieving because of the court case about her death

THE DILEMMAS OF IDENTITY

Who am I now?

What is the point of me?

Is there a name for a mother without a child?

I cannot be both a mother and a father

I will never be a granny now

I am an orphan now

I am the head of the family now – I don't want that responsibility

How can I ever fill the space my sister left for my parents?

I think Mum is looking to me to be a replacement husband and look after her but I don't want to

I feel compelled to be more attentive to my parents since my sister's death

I no longer feel like a child – I finally feel like a grown up

The favourite child died

I am an only child now

I have a family but not my birth family – it is such a loss

Am I still a wife even if I don't have a husband?

Am I still a mother after my child/children died?

I don't like not being part of a couple

Can I still call myself Mrs or am I now Ms?

Can anybody see me?

Can you fix me?

Will people think I was the cause of her suicide?

Because he was murdered, we have to read half-truths in the press about our family and him

I feel so vulnerable – I never felt like that before

I feel so alone

I am purposeless now

I feel like I have had an amputation

I feel like I have been cut in two

Now I am labelled 'newly bereaved'

What does being a widow/widower mean exactly?

Will anyone want me again?

Will anyone ever think I am sexy again?

I feel like an outcast

Will workmen take advantage of me as a woman alone?

People are different with me now – they just think 'poor me'

We weren't married and it appears I have no rights

As the mistress, I was not allowed to go to the funeral – it was so cruel

People think I am ready to date – far from it, he might be dead but I am still married to him

I haven't told anyone at work she died because I didn't want them to treat me differently

I am searching for something

THE SPIRITUAL MEANING

The funeral is so important – it means a lot to give him a good send off

God has abandoned me

I pray all the time

I have stopped praying

I feel punished by God

Do you believe in heaven and hell?

Why did this happen to us?

I don't know why I am here

What does death actually mean?

What is it all for?

I had a dream about her

I've got to get the headstone right – it means so much

I've put some of her ashes in all the places we have loved

I am going to see a medium

Do you believe in life after death?

I am frightened of my mother's spirit – she haunts me

I've made an altar in the sitting room with all his special things

There is a shrine for her beside the spot where she was killed

I keep hearing 'our song' – I think he is doing it for me

He comes to me at night and sits on the bed – he lay down next to me once

There's a robin which comes at all the important moments – it is him

A butterfly flew out of the window after she died

When I see a white feather, I know it's a sign

I listen to beautiful music to feel close to her

I tattooed his name on my wrist so he is always with me

I've started writing poetry to express how I feel

My tears are a deep connection to him

My tears say the words I cannot speak

My grief is how I honour our love

The work he did has made the world a better place

We let off Chinese lanterns on the anniversary with messages tied to them

I light a candle for him every night

I know he is that bright star that you can see

She was my soul mate

His soul lives on

What if his soul is angry with me?

You can never take away the love

Even though I only held her for a brief time, she brought me joy (and sadness)

To have been loved that much is something really special

What does death
actually mean?

CHAPTER 5
A DESOLATE PLACE

The wave has done its worst and what is left in its wake is an irrevocably changed beach, where you may find yourself walking in totally unfamiliar territory. During this time, navigating your way round the changed landscape of your life can feel impossible, overwhelming and desperately difficult.

You don't quite know how to plot your course and you cannot yet see the path ahead of you.

I will never get over this

People keep asking me if I am OK now

My friends ask if I have 'got over it' … NO!

Everything feels wrong

Some days are OK, then I find myself on the floor again

I don't want this

I can't cope

I am overwhelmed

I'm so lonely

I want him back

I long to meet her in my dreams

When I go into my house at night, I check every room in case he is there

I keep thinking I will see her

When I'm at home I want to be in our flat by the sea and when I am there I want to be at home

I can't bear driving in the dark any more

I have lost my confidence about everything

There is already infighting in the family over the will

Probate takes forever

I worry I'll get things wrong

It's so hard to make decisions

I have no-one to talk it through with

I spend all weekend on my own – I don't see a soul

Only people who've lost someone understand me

I need antidepressants

I do not want to be put on antidepressants

I don't want any help – I can do this on my own

I feel helpless

I'll need counselling for ever

My friends were great at the beginning but they've all drifted away now (except one)

I think my friends are bored by me now

Someone told me "grief will rearrange my address book" and it's true

It seems grief lasts longer than sympathy

It feels like one step forward and two steps backwards

There's no point cooking any more

I can't go out with other couples

I don't want to see couples holding hands or listen to their plans

I want to be alone to grieve

I thought I saw him today but it wasn't him and this plunged me straight back

I can/can't hear her voice in my head

I'm not going to change my answerphone message, even though my friends think I should

I seem to have lost confidence in my parenting skills

My children are getting on my nerves

Shouldn't I be feeling better by now?

I feel so guilty when I laugh or have fun

My friends think I should start dating

I am dating

I have met someone who is really kind and supportive

Men seem very interested in me and my widow status but I am not ready

I felt so guilty when I had sex for the first time with my new partner but she understood

I know I am being promiscuous but it feels good to be wanted again

I'll never marry again

I want another baby

I keep crying at work

I want answers from the GP/doctors/hospital/nurses/midwife/coroners/police

I cannot start to grieve till the inquest is over

Life will never be
the same again

I want my old life back

I am so angry with...

My moods are all over the place

I regret not asking all the questions I harboured – I didn't dare

Now I will never know the answers

I am so irritable all the time

I cried inside when I realised everyone had their Dad there, except me

I am furious and so jealous of others who have their Mum

I just lie on the sofa and time passes by

I know I am drinking too much at the moment

We are clearing the house out – it's so painful, so many memories

My sister wants to get rid of Mum's clothes but I can't let them go

We can't decide what to do with the ashes

I redecorated the bedroom, which I regretted and cried all day

I can't make any changes because what would it mean that I have moved on

I still cannot read books or listen to music

Why do my appliances break or just stop working?

What will happen if I become ill – who will look after me?

I've got pains in my tummy – do you think I've got cancer too?

The friends I thought I could rely on have evaporated

The least likely friend has been very supportive – it is so unexpected

I know a lot of time has passed but I still can't accept he is dead

The anniversary of her final diagnosis is next week – it is all so vivid

I am absolutely dreading the anniversary of his death

In retrospect, the mortuary viewing made it real

I want to put him on a pedestal in the sky because I feel people are forgetting him

Some days are OK, then it hits me again

CHAPTER 6

STARTING TO BUILD A NEW LIFE AFTER THE TSUNAMI

Gradually you find yourself able to muster the energy to clear a path through the flotsam and jetsam of your desolated beach. You are becoming more familiar with the contours of the shifted sands. A way forward gradually begins to appear. You may find yourself moving forward on this path but at times turning back to the beach again.

This is natural and normal.

INTELLECTUAL UNDERSTANDING

I didn't realise that grief is such hard work

I now know I will never see him again

I know she is dead but it has been hard to believe it

I know I can manage, even if I would prefer not to

I'm getting used to it all

It's taken a really long time

I am stronger than I thought

I am more resilient than I thought

I realise I can make good decisions for the family

I can't believe a year (or two) has passed but life goes on

EMOTIONAL ACCEPTANCE

I don't beat myself up if I remember I haven't thought of her for a few hours/days

I know I will have bad days but they will pass

I am less anxious now

I feel comfortable at home again

I still miss her but it feels less raw

The upsetting images of his death have receded and they are replaced with happy memories

I don't cry so much – I laugh more often

I just take each day as it comes

I don't worry about little things anymore

I feel more 'normal'

I don't want grief to become a habit

PRACTICAL REORGANISATION

I can do more than I ever thought, though it is tiring

My job's a godsend

I still put my make up on and dress nicely – he would want me to

I'm accepting invitations, even if I just stay a while

I've booked a holiday

I'm driving longer distances

I can fill the car up with petrol and get it serviced

I'm keeping busy with my grandchildren

I visited a friend up north – I've never been this far from home

I went on the train on my own

I'm taking pleasure in nature, walking in the woods

I am looking after myself better now

I can listen to music we liked now

I've changed my job so I can look after my children

I've started some volunteer work

I am more attentive to my children/parents

I plan something special to do for our wedding anniversary and her birthday

I cook properly again

I keep busy – it really helps

I'm asking for help now
when I need it

ENGAGING WITH NEW RELATIONSHIPS

I now know who my real friends are – I treasure that

I don't want to marry again but I can be single, although I didn't think it was possible

I've met someone

I am going to remarry but I feel like a bigamist – I still love my first wife very much

I'm pregnant

I talk to my children more

I have made new friends he never knew

SLOWLY MOVING FORWARD WHILE METAPHORICALLY BRINGING YOUR BELOVED WITH YOU

When I have a problem, I think of him and somehow I know what to do

I think of her every day – she is always with me

I carry him in my heart

I do what is right for my soul now

I will never get over her but I think it is going to be OK at some point

The memories are so precious

I remember him in flashes

I loved him in my bones – I can't let go of that

I am not going to move on without her – I will 'bring her' with me wherever life takes me

I am a different person to the one I was and I rather like him

CHAPTER 7
THE NEW NORMAL

Your beach has gradually come back to life. Whilst the sands have shifted and the patterns have altered, the pebbles, shells and seaweed once more line the sea shore, as if nothing had ever happened.

Yet you know something did happen and the core of your being has been shaken. What you may have taken for granted before, has come back into focus and you look at life through a different lens now and it holds more meaning. You notice that the sea grasses are waving again and the sky seems brighter. Once again you hear the waves and the seagulls and you inhale the tang of the salty sea air more deeply.

You can see that you and your life have expanded around your grief in ways you could not have anticipated previously. Without you even realising it, this altered beach has slowly and painstakingly revealed itself to you as your new normal. As you look across the sea, you feel open to what is yet to come.

I am still alive

I even plan ahead now

I am just a little bit proud of myself

The worst has happened to me – I can cope with anything now

I have come such a long way

I am making a life of my own

That period of my life is behind me now

From being a couple, a new independent me has emerged

I could not have done it without support

I have made really good connections with other widowers

I laugh again without feeling guilty

I feel happiness again

I didn't know I had it in me

I have grown as a person

I have learned so much

I am confident in the new me

I love learning new things

I have my energy back

I kept his business going and discovered a new me inside

I trust myself

I like myself

I am stronger

I feel more peaceful

I still cry and I allow myself to cry when I need to

It's my grief and mine alone to feel whenever I want to

I am deeply grateful for all the love, care and attention I have received

My life has grown around my grief

I can listen to other people's problems again

I am moving forward with him in my heart

I have finally got used to him being dead

Missing her is still important to me – it is a connection to her

Grief has grown up alongside me my whole life

I hear his voice in my head and I know what to do

The aloneness does not feel lonely any more

I am gradually realising I could love again

Keeping his photograph on display is important, despite my new relationship

He is stitched into the fabric of my life

Once again, desire and passion is part of my life

My new partner is very different but so am I

I thought moving on felt very scary – now I know I don't have to move on if I don't want to

No one can tell me what to do anymore

I feel a freedom I never had

I have made new friends he never knew

Only now do I understand the grief of my bereaved friends

You don't only grieve for the person, you grieve everything you would have done with them

I now realise the value of deep grief

'The gift of death,' I know what that means now and finally I feel grown up

There are no ground rules for grief

There is no time limit to grief

It is true, it does get better

I have survived

CHAPTER 8

REMEMBERING

Remembering is a very private and intimate way of reconnecting with the person you have lost. It is a strange thing but sometimes you can yearn to remember something and it does not come into view, then other times there will be a trigger, such as a smell, a tune, a place, a taste or a word, which suddenly transports you back and it is as if the person who died is with you again.

When a long time has passed since the death and everyone has gone back to their busy lives, you may find your grief is forgotten by the majority. That is why memories become so precious because you can spend as long as you want immersed in your recollections and your feelings.

Sometimes our minds and hearts box up memories and keep them buried because they feel too sad, too frightening or too difficult. Maybe you don't know how you would handle them? You might find that as the years go by, you are able to lift the lid on that 'box' and have a look at the memories. You may discover that you have grown in so many different ways since the death that you find yourself able to cope with them from a stronger place.

Memories can serve as an anchor for you to hold onto for the rest of your own life. That is the wonderful thing about them.

Memories link our
past to my present

MEMORIES

I don't want anyone to tell me differently – these are my memories

My memories are beautiful and so bittersweet

Memories can be upsetting or soothing – it just depends on my day

Those memories are mine and mine alone

No-one can touch my memories

My memory of my parents is sacred

Memories can knock the wind out of your sails, like a blow to the stomach

I can't wait for quiet days, just so I can have a day to reminisce

My memories take away the harshness of her death and make it softer

My body still tingles when I remember our lovemaking

Certain music will allow me to merge with the memories of him

While I am alive, I am the keeper of the memories of her and of her own memories

I felt the gone-ness so badly but now I see he is never gone

I have these lovely dreams of her in which I see her so clearly

I remember every little detail

Poignant memories make me sad but bring me infinitely closer to my father

Sometimes when I remember something, I write it down quickly so I don't forget

Everything in her house holds a memory

DIFFICULT MEMORIES

I still feel the wound of being orphaned – it never leaves me

My body remembers her

I have had years of anxious feelings in my stomach when I think of some memories

I am an expert in remembering the longing, the missing and the yearning

No-one knows I had a brother

There are no memories of my sister – she died before I was born

We were not allowed to talk about my brother after he died

I was ten and at primary school, so at my new secondary school no-one knew

My memories are of illness, illness, illness and then dead and gone

I haven't ever talked about it until now

He took his own life – we weren't allowed to talk about it and that hurt me

He was gay and died of AIDS – everyone is trying to forget that

There were so many dead. How can I remember just one? It would be wrong

The memories are too painful, too raw – I won't go there

I am so frightened because my memories are fading

It seemed safer not to talk about that time – now I am not so sure

No-one asked me about him

I was so young when it happened – why do I feel so discombobulated now?

Surely you cannot feel a memory when you have no memory?

My body is primed for the unexpected

That glimpse of him in someone else's face brought memories crashing in

Time has stood still for me – I pretend I'm OK but I cannot forget it all

Memories are for others, not me

I froze in time the day he died

Will I remember her in years to come?

I don't ever want to think of him, let alone have memories

He's buried for good, as are the memories with him

I have no memory of him, just a very uncomfortable feeling

I hate having flashbacks – they unsettle me for days

I needed to find a place without all these painful memories

I feel guilty because I am the one who survived

Why do I never have any dreams of her?

Everyone in my family has different memories of the same thing

I remember the good
and the bad,
she was only human

WISHFUL MEMORIES

They would want me to...

I wish she could have lived for ever

I have created a memory that my Dad is walking me down the aisle

In my mind she is still that same little girl

I think of my Dad as a hero but I know he wasn't really

I know I have put my Mum on a pedestal in my memories

I wonder what my Mum would have said

I wonder what my Dad would have done

I so wish my children could have known their grandparents

I create a fantasy world around me in which we are both very much alive

I imagine my Dad with my firstborn in his arms – he would have been so proud

I pictured my Mum with all the others mums at sports day, cheering me on

In my dreams, we are the perfect family

It seems like everyone has forgotten my parents – I don't want them erased

CHAPTER 9

WHO CAN HELP ME?

We know how difficult it is to ask for help, especially when you feel at your lowest ebb. In grief, you can end up feeling extremely isolated from the world. It can feel as though the world goes on as if nothing has happened. There are many reasons that might inhibit you from asking for the support you need, at a time when you really do need help.

Though it may not occur to you at the moment, if you felt able to reach out, there are people who want to offer their assistance, support and encouragement at this time. Think of it this way, wouldn't you want to help support someone you care about if they were grieving?

WHO CAN HELP?

People who have been bereaved

Particularly people who have been bereaved in similar circumstances

Family members

Friends

Employers/colleagues

Neighbours

GP/health workers

School teachers

College tutors

University counselling teams

Religious communities

Spiritual churches

Mediums

Shamans/healers

Hospital or hospice chaplains

The unexpected person

The Samaritans

Home help or carer

Bereavement counsellors

Bereavement support groups

Pets

Fellow gardeners and walkers

You, offering support to others in the same situation, in the future

What Do I Need?

Write what you need on this page:

CHAPTER 10

FOR THOSE SUPPORTING THE BEREAVED: WHAT SUPPORT IS HELPFUL AND WHAT IS NOT?

We know from our work with the bereaved that small things can make a huge difference. Can you be brave enough to be the one who steps towards the bereaved, acknowledge their loss and offer warmth, love and practical help? Are you able to hold their gaze for just a few seconds longer to demonstrate your solidarity alongside them, in their grief? In that moment, you are showing them that you can endure their pain, instead of acting on an urge to fix it or take it away.

Friends and wider family can feel very inadequate after a death but doing something to help gives one a purpose and is very caring and supportive for the bereaved. Here are some ideas to inspire you. You don't have to do them all, just pick one or two to begin with.

hold the hope

throw a life belt

give your time

be their rock

hear their waves

be their wing.

be a harbour

be patient

be their anchor

If you don't know what to say, try one of these...

I don't know what to say

It is terribly sad

What happened?

How are you feeling today?

Tell me about it

Would you like to talk?

What can I do?

Are you happy for me to do ... for you?

WHAT HELPS IN THE SHORTER TERM

Give of your time

Use the deceased's name liberally in the conversation

Allow your friend to cry

Don't assume the bereaved person will cry

Listen without judgment

Speak regularly with your bereaved employee

Offer a structured route for returning back to work

Remember there is no rule book and no time frame for grief

Be patient when they want to tell you their story over and over again

Understand that composure is overrated

Don't pretend that nothing has happened

Grief is exhausting – acknowledge their tiredness and encourage resting

Be aware that you may subconsciously pick up and feel the bereaved person's mood – it is not yours

Give them time to reconnect when they have been deep in thought

A gentle touch or a hug goes a long way

Quietly observe the change in their face in the early weeks – it will show all the signs of someone in shock

Cook a meal ready to serve and take it round to their house

Cook meals for the freezer with clear instructions

Make a shopping list, shop and put away the shopping

Follow up and follow through on what you have offered

Keep asking the
bereaved out,
even if they say no

Try and protect them from the people who, sadly, take advantage of the newly bereaved

Accompany them to the funeral directors/inquest/ GP/hospital appointments etc.

Take the children out for some fun time (children need reprieve from grief)

Keep getting in touch, thereby not isolating the bereaved person

Suggest making a memory box, photo collage or book – you could do it with them

Make a playlist of meaningful music for the family

Be the designated driver

Try and take them into the great outdoors – fresh air and nature are good for the soul

Take their dog for a walk

Don't be surprised if there is laughter – there is humour in the midst of grief

See the person underneath the mask called 'I am trying to cope'

Don't assume that others will be there to help – you may be the only person who has offered so far

Receiving a proper letter of condolence and not a Facebook message, makes all the difference

Can you help them write letters of appreciation or thank-you letters?

Expect the person to express a lot of different feelings

Be prepared for outbursts of anger – it is not personal

Acknowledge how angry the person is – you do not need to fix it

WHAT HELPS IN THE LONGER TERM

Understanding:

The second year is often harder for the bereaved

It may take years for the bereaved to begin to feel better, when they have loved deeply

That they generally feel safest in their own home

Don't be annoyed if they want to leave a get-together early – they often need a 'get-out clause'

The bereaved have the right to change their mind

Be accepting of the new person they have become – they had no choice but to adapt and grow

Their grief continues to be unique to them and them alone

Encourage the bereaved not to compare their grief to others

No one person or a single theory can define their grief

Doing:

Remember the important dates such as: the date of the death, birthdays and anniversaries, especially in the second year when all the first special dates come around again

Surf the web for supportive websites (see chapter 11)

Set up an In Memoriam page

Help plan a Memorial Service

Tell them your stories about their loved one – it keeps the beloved present and remembered

If you have photos or video clips they haven't seen, make copies and send them

Start a blog for family and friends as a place to share grief

Suggest books that you think may speak to the bereaved person's experience

Suggest they turn to the arts for comfort: poetry, music, film, books, art and quotations

Suggest the person creates a sanctuary, safe haven or shrine in their home to retreat to

If they are struggling with unsaid things, suggest they write a letter to their loved one expressing what they wished they had said

Help them maintain the garden – consider a memorial bench with a plaque

How can you assist with easing the household tasks, e.g. administration?

Help to sort out the digital footprint (Twitter, Facebook, Instagram, Pinterest, LinkedIn, Tumblr, Snap-chat, Gmail, Yahoo, Hotmail, AOL, PayPal and any others) of the deceased

www.modernloss.com has an excellent article about this subject under the 'How To' section: Getting Dead Loved Ones Offline

Suggest the person keeps a journal and writes down precious memories because they might fade

You could ask your friends to write down their memories of the deceased

Visit the home instead of phoning or texting

Can you stay over and cook a meal so the person can get some rest and eats properly?

You can help plan special activities to acknowledge the important dates for the person

Plan a visit to a meaningful place

Take them to the cemetery or crematorium if they want to go

Suggest they wear something belonging to the deceased – it is comforting

Suggest a local support group

Suggest seeking the help of a counsellor – talking therapies can help

Encourage them to lean into their grief – it is harmful not to

Talk about safety checks with them, now that they are on their own

Encourage them to say "no" if they don't want to do something but feel they ought to

Honour the person who has died through a social or community event like a sponsored walk

Donate to a cause close to the heart of the person who died

Would they like to write a list of qualities the deceased has passed on to them?

Suggest sensitively that you are willing to help whenever they are ready to sort the deceased's belongings

Help them focus on priorities for the here and now

Be gracious

WHAT IS NOT HELPFUL

Avoid clichés and inadvertent hurtful advice, such as:

You are doing so well

I know how you feel

It is a blessing

You can still have other children

You are the man of the house now

Death is something we don't talk about

Don't talk about her, you'll get upset

You will feel better in a few months

You must be over it by now

Time heals

Put the past behind you

Try to look for the positive

Don't cry – he or she wouldn't want you to

He is in a better place

Everything will be ok

You are still young – you will marry again

At least they are no longer in pain

You have your life ahead of you

You can get a new pet

At least she had a long life

There is a reason for everything

She is in God's hands now

Give it time, you will get over it

You can have closure now

Don't talk about your own losses

Don't compare – each bereavement has its own landscape

Don't avoid mentioning the deceased or using their name

Don't be afraid to mention the words 'died', 'dead', 'death'

Don't proselytise your own religion or beliefs

Don't feel hurt if your friend rebuffs your offers – sometimes the bereaved need to be alone

Don't stop the bereaved talking about their loved one repeatedly – they still need to do this

Don't relate stories about similar deaths

Don't touch or throw away anything without asking – you don't know what memory clings to that particular object

Don't suggest they need to sort out the ashes right away – they don't

Don't pressurise the bereaved to go back to work before they are ready

Don't leave the return to work open-ended either

Don't cross the road when you see the bereaved person coming towards you

Don't judge when a bereaved person starts a new life – they'd rather have their loved one back any day

Don't be jealous when a bereaved friend is able to go on long trips now

When I look back,
I can't believe how
far I've come

CHAPTER 11

USEFUL RESOURCES

In our experience many people find solace in the use of social media, the internet and organisations specialising in bereavement. We hope you will find what it is you need. There is much more support out there waiting to be discovered.

EMERGENCY HELP WHEN IN DESPAIR

www.samaritans.org

HOW TO FIND A BEREAVEMENT COUNSELLOR OR BEREAVEMENT SUPPORT

www.bacp.co.uk/about-therapy/how-to-find-a-therapist

www.counselling-directory.org.uk

www.cruse.org.uk

www.careforthefamily.org.uk

www.modernloss.com

www.gov.uk/after-a-death/organisations-you-need-to-contact-and-tell-us-once

www.mywishes.co.uk

FORUMS

www.widowedandyoung.org.uk

www.way-up.co.uk

SUPPORT FOR THOSE AFFECTED BY SUICIDE

www.uksobs.org

www.allianceofhope.org

SUPPORT FOR CHILDREN OR YOUNG PEOPLE WHO HAVE LOST A LOVED ONE

www.childhoodbereavementnetwork.org.uk

www.childbereavementuk.org

www.winstonswish.org

SUPPORT FOR PARENTS AND FAMILY AFTER THE BIRTH OF A STILLBORN BABY OR THE DEATH OF A BABY OR CHILD

www.miscarriageassociation.org.uk

www.sands.org.uk

www.lullabytrust.org.uk

www.childbereavementuk.org

www.tcf.org.uk

www.childdeathhelpline.org.uk

FOR YOUNG PEOPLE

www.hopeagain.org.uk

www.griefencounter.org.uk

SUPPORT FOR THOSE AFFECTED BY MURDER AND MANSLAUGHTER

www.samm.org.uk

WHEN YOUR PET HAS DIED

www.bluecross.org.uk

FOR THOSE SUFFERING FROM DEPRESSION AND ANXIETY

www.mind.org.uk

FOR EMPLOYERS

www.beta.acas.org.uk

(ACAS: Advisory, Conciliation and Arbitration Service)

TWITTER

There are many useful grief sites on Twitter. Just put the word 'grief' into the search bar

GRIEF MEMOIRS

A Grief Observed by C. S. Lewis

Can I Let You Go, My Love by Kay van Dijk

Grief Is The Thing With Feathers by Max Porter

Widow to Widow, Thoughtful, Practical Ideas for Rebuilding Your Life by Genevieve Davis Ginsburg

The Great Below, A Journey into Loss by Maddy Paxman

Living On the Seabed, a Memoir of Love, Life and Survival by Lindsay Nicholson

The Year of Magical Thinking by Joan Didion

Saturday Night Widows, The Adventures of Six Friends Remaking Their Lives by Becky Aikman

When Breath Becomes Air by Paul Kalanithi

BOOKS FOR MEN

Parenting with Balls by Ian Newbold

Men & Grief, A Guide for Men Surviving the Death of a Loved One by Carol Staudacher

Grieving Dads, To the Brink and Back by Kelly Farley with David DiCola

Thinking Out Loud by Rio Ferdinand

SPECIFIC SUBJECT BOOKS

The Empty Bed, Bereavement and the Loss of Love by Susan Wallbank

The Lone Twin, Understanding Twin Bereavement and Loss by Joan Woodward

The Other Side of Complicated Grief: Hope in the Midst of Despair by Rhonda O'Neill

Grief in Young Children, A Handbook for Adults by Atle Dyregrov

A Special Scar, 2nd Edition: The Experiences of People Bereaved by Suicide by Alison Wertheimer

HELP TO HEAL FROM GRIEF BOOKS

It's OK That You're Not OK: Meeting Grief and Loss in a Culture That Doesn't Understand by Megan Devine

Grief Works, Stories of Life, Death and Surviving by Julia Samuel

Honouring Grief – Creating a Space to Let Yourself Heal by Alexandra Kennedy

Mindfulness & the Journey of Bereavement, Restoring Hope after a Death by Peter Bridgewater

Healing a Friend's Grieving Heart, 100 Practical Ideas by Alan D. Wolfelt

All Alan D. Wolfelt's books which cover teens, adults, spouses, parents, siblings, trauma, stillbirth and suicide

Wendelien (left) and Katrina (right) – Photograph by Gary Fielder

ABOUT THE
AUTHORS AND ILLUSTRATOR

Wendelien McNicoll BACP (Snr. Accred) is an experienced Counsellor and Supervisor with a Private Practice, specialised in palliative and bereavement counselling. Her career started at Thames Hospice where she gained insight into all aspects of the end of life journey, from volunteer counsellor to trustee. She trained as a Soul Midwife with Felicity Warner. She facilitates Death Cafés in her area to encourage the conversation around death and dying.

Katrina Taee was a counsellor specialising in grief for 17 years. She spent 11 years working as a volunteer counsellor at Thames Hospice alongside running a private practice. She has blogged about grief through her website to help the bereaved. She has now trained as an End of Life Doula with Living Well Dying Well and is a member of End of Life Doula UK. Her years of working with grief fold naturally in with her end of life work.

Ruth Thorp is a designer and illustrator based in Bath where she runs Ruth Thorp Studio full-time. She creates a range of illustrated products and collaborates on other creative projects and commissions. She has published three picture books and produced cover art, book illustrations and editorial artwork for a range of publications. She has a degree in Architecture. www.ruththorpstudio.co.uk